Foreword

Jennifer is a well known local artist who also loves music and some of the 'poems' were originally written as folk songs.

She is not Cornish but married a Hocking from Gorran Haven and wishes to thank the late Archie Smith, James Whetter and Phillip Payton (in his historical notes of Cornwall) and many locals who gave personal insights into a way of life, now gone.

The Clay Mines

The ports around the St Austell Bay were very busy loading clay to sailing ships and, later, cargo boats in the 19th and 20th centuries. This is about the working of the clay mines and the information given to me by several people who worked (or their fathers/mothers) in the St Austell area.

Up upon the Cornish moorland, near St Austell town,
hills of white can be seen where clay was found,
but long before that Quaker man discovered kaolin
the only work was mining of the tin.
Charlestown and Pentewan, Par and Fowey ports -
they were always busy with the local fish they caught;
later they were crowded with the sailing ships galore
shipping out the china clay and ore.

Coopers skilled in making barrels for the china clay
worked long hours in the mills for very little pay;
binding up the wooden casks with supple withies, light,
to seal them up and keep them watertight.
Blacksmith's shops a-plenty for beating out the spades;
forging iron frames for carts and horses' shoes were made;
carpenters repaired the shovels
and made the wheels and skips
and wagons, strong, for loading up the tips.

Strong young men would break the burden
digging at the clay;
older men in 'streamers' boots washed the stones away.
Hawsers pulled the over-burden up the tips and then
'twas emptied out by the winder men.
'Darby Clogs' the footwear, for wearing in the dries;
clay was marked in lines to cut in blocks, then stored inside.
In the kiln the heavy clothing wore out in the heat
from the fires beneath their feet.

Blocks of clay, when stored in driers, turned a little green;
young 'Bal maids' wearing the 'Gooks',
scraped to keep them clean.
'Kettle boys' would grease the rails
and make the welcome tea;
'captains' were the ones to oversee.
Teams of handsome horses pulled the heavy drays
down the hills to little ports around St Austell bay;
the sailing ships were loaded with the valued white cargo -
in the days not so long ago.

The Cornish Fisherman

Many years ago the fishing was done in small coves and the pilchard shoals were pulled up onto the beach with huge nets by lots of villagers. The 'Huers' stood on the cliffs and when they spotted the huge shoals of pilchards they would wave furze (gorse) branches to signal to where the pilchards were. Later fishermen used boats to catch different fish because the large trawlers over-fished the pilchards.

In years gone by the fishermen were many in the bay,
and village life was centred round the catches of the day.
The fish then were a-plenty, so he had a heavy net,
and he would brave the stormy seas
for the catches he could get.

>The seas are unpredictable
>when they are far from land,
>but there's no one knows the waters like
>a Cornish fisherman.

From summer to December the pilchard shoals came by
and the 'Huers' on the clifftops would wave the furze and cry.
The waiting boats would circle round
to trap them in the seine
and all would pull the heaving nets up on the shore again.

Then came the Northern 'drifters' to fish among our shores;
they over-fished our waters, and pilchards came no more,
so, men made large herring boats with many a sturdy crew
to sail around all England, to catch the fish so few.

The crabbing boats were never meant to fish in waters deep,
and bigger boats smash up the crabs,
"'tis only toes they keep"
and, though the cod are plenty,
they must return them to the sea,
but Frenchmen are allowed to keep 'a better haul than we!'

So, men are forced to sell their boats or turn to tourist trade,
and many regulations make it difficult today;
they really need to change the fishing quotas for our seas
or fishing here in Cornwall may soon forever cease.

> The seas are unpredictable
> when they are far from land,
> but there's no one knows the waters like
> a Cornish fisherman.

What A Night!

This is about a young fisherman who has gone out with the fleet and they have had a wonderful catch and so they will be welcomed home by one-and-all, especially his young wife!

What a night it has been
as we went with the tide,
out in the curve of the bay with our nets floating wide;
with a wind from the South
blowing steadily,
clear and starry as far as we could see.

What a catch we have had,
hauling all through the night,
riding the crests of the waves till the first morning light.
Heavy laden our fleet,
far off from the shore,
we have herring and mullet, pilchards and more!

What a sunrise at dawn
when it coloured the day,
checking our haul and our nets as we sat in the bay;
then we headed for home
knowing there would be
someone patiently watching and waiting for me.

What a rest we will have
from our labours, as we
tend to our boats in the warm morning sun on the quay,
and tomorrow our fleet,
whether sun or rain,
plies the Channel til safely home again.

What a night! What a night it has been!

Cliff Primroses, Cornwall

*In Spring we went for a walk along the cliffs on the North
Coast to try and blow away the cobwebs and boredom of
everyday life and by the time we came home, we felt
renewed.*

The wind was blowing chill and strong
on our pathway to the sea,
whilst April sunshine, bright and clear
warmed valleys in the lee.
Stunted grasses, heathers too,
grew in the salty air,
though rugged cliffs and shaley soil
gave little shelter there.

We turned inland a little space
and there, to our surprise,
tucked behind a stony wall
(and on the northern side),
banks and banks of primroses,
delicately hued,
bursting forth their dainty heads
to greet the day anew.

How can those flowers flourish there
where tempests often blow,
upon those wild Atlantic shores
where little else will grow?
They little knew what sheer delight
their presence gave us then;
our hearts uplifted, home we went
to face the world again.

The Kittiwake

We like the cliffs at Newquay. I sat there for a while, feeling a little 'blue'. So I watched the seabirds, dipping and diving, and one of them flew past, very close to me and looked me right in the eye! It was quite an experience.

Wheeling, dipping, slowly turning,
lifted high and free,
a kittiwake came skimming past
o'er the cliffs beside the sea.
There on a rocky face he stopped
at his nest, tucked in the lee.

A moments pause and off he went -
on a gust of wind he soared;
down, down he dropped with joyous cry
towards the sandy shore;
a bright, shrill call, a flap of wings,
then back to his nest once more.

Again he rose up gracefully,
just hanging in the air,
then swooping down, he circled round
and saw me watching there;
he drifted past and gazed at me -
a level, studied stare.

How beautiful, that snowy bird,
as he went gliding by.
He seemed to draw me to clouds
as he floated in the sky.
My spirits rose, along with him,
I felt that I could fly.

The First Rose

*One morning I got up with a sigh and thought of all the jobs
that needed doing around the garden. Then, I opened the
back door and there I saw the first rose of the year!*

There it was! To my delight,
sheltered from the cold at night,
I barely saw it nestled there,
blood red it was and shaped so fair -
a perfect rose!

Beside the sill, alone it grew;
scented petals fresh with dew.
Its brightness caught my careless eye,
I very nearly passed it by -
that lovely rose.

God's gift to me, this rose, today;
tucked behind a leaf it lay and
warmed by springtime's gentle sun,
it seemed to herald, "Summer's come!"
The first May rose.

There's Plenty More Fish
In The Sea

*This is about a woman (not in the first flush of youth!) who is
fed up working in the cannery in Mevagissey in the early/mid
20th century and wants a better life than cleaning and gutting
fish and feels she should have one.*

When Oi was young I loved to see
the fishin' boats tied to the quay;
shouted greetings from busy men,
for they had bigger catches then;
loaded mauns
and fishy smells,
the shrieks and cries of the gulls as well.
  It was fish, fish, fish every day for me,
   and there's plenty more fish in the sea.

Moi mother found a job for me
cleanin' fish in the cannery;
Working for hours till moi hands was sore -
wooden clogs on my feet Oi wore.
Frozen fingers
gutting fish;
well, 'twas not the kind of life oi wished.

A fishmonger in our little town
wanted a wife to settle down;
'e fancied me, it was quite plain, then
'e asked to marry me once again,
but said if 'e
can't marry me -
then there were plenty more fish in the sea.

'E wouldn't wait for long Oi feared and
it was the first chance Oi'd 'ad in years!
'Though he was stout and a little old -
Oi'm no oil paintin', so Oi've bin told.
'E 'ad a shop
and a nice cottage too, so
Oi thought it might be the best thing to do.
     It was fish, fish, fish every day for me
     and there's plenty more fish in the sea.

A difficult choice it was for me, but
Oi'd 'ad enough of the cannery.
Moi mother said, "'E seems quite nice
and if you'll take moi advice -
You should wed
if you can, for
I know that 'e's quite a wealthy man.

So oi did what moi mother said
and the fishmonger and Oi was wed.
Oi thought Oi'd have a life of ease
but e's a difficult man to please.
Oi mind the shop
now Oi'm 'is wife, and
oi cut up fish every day of moi life!
     It's still fish, fish, fish every day for me
     and there's plenty more fish in the sea!!

A Summer's Eve

When I lived at Gorran Haven I used to stroll down to the quay in a late summer evening and loved the sounds at that time of day just as the sun was setting in the western skies.

Leaning on the harbour wall
I saw the first star twinkling;
brightly hued in skies of gold -
the summer sun was sinking.
Painted boats were moored below
with many roped together,
sheltering within the quay
away from stormy weather, weather,
away from stormy weather.

Feeling cool upon my face
were Southern breezes playing;
in the darkened pools below
the seaweed gently swaying.
Farther out into the bay
I watch the seabirds dipping -
following the little boat
homeward from its fishing, fishing,
homeward from its fishing.

Children leaping from the quay
With shouts of merry laughter;
mem'ries of that summer's eve will
linger ever after.
Voices hung upon the air,
with the seagulls blended.
Violet the evening sky
as home, my way I wended, wended,
as home, my way I wended.

Upon The Cliff Tops

One day I was sitting up on the cliffs watching all the activity down below in the harbour and all the sea sports racing around in the bay, and I thought, "Isn't this wonderful - I can just sit here and watch all this and do absolutely nothing!"

A day on the cliff tops, alone, with the ocean below;
watching the waves on the sand as they ripple and flow;
translucent pools
left on the rocks,
inviting and cool - inviting and cool.

Dipping and wheeling the kittiwakes call as they fly -
back to their young in the nests on the ledges nearby.
Ochre and grey
colour the cliffs
edging the bay - edging the bay.

Red-gold the montbretia grows by the low hawthorn trees.
Bright ox-eyed daises are waving their heads in the breeze.
Tucked in the lee
tiny wild flowers
hang o'er the sea - hang o'er the sea.

Out on the misty horizon the sailboats pass by -
little dark silhouettes, under the blue of the sky.
Diamonds bright
flash on the waves
in the sunlight - in the sunlight.

Up from the beaches come sounds of the people at play.
The throb of the motorboats taking their tours round the bay.
Out in the haze
skiers speed by
but, here, I laze - but, here, I laze!

The Wreck Of The Pallas Of Vasa in 1895

The Pallas of Vasa was wrecked off Gorran Haven bay and because there were many brandy kegs on board (some of which were washed up on the 'finders-keeper's' beach and others winched up to the cliffs) there ended up a free-for-all to get at the brandy first!

In a cold November, heading Bristol way,
a brigantine in heavy sail crossed St Austell Bay
with a cargo from the Baltic -
brandy and pitch pine.
The wind was blowing hard and strong
although the day was fine.

   The brigantine then foundered on that fateful day.
  The ship was broken on the Yaw in Gorran Haven bay.

The Captain's beard was ginger, a sturdy Swedish man.
He lost his bearings to the West
and veered towards the land.
He loved his tot of brandy and
he'd had quite a few.
He steered his ship on the Gwineas rock
and broke the keel in two.

The Coastguard saw the wrecking -
the Breeches Buoy was called;
They winched some sailors up the cliff
and brandy kegs were hauled.
To stop the people squabbling,
and there was quite a fray,
an elder opened up a keg
and poured it in the bay!

The brigantine then foundered on that fateful day.
The ship was broken on the Yaw in Gorran Haven bay.

Then some of the barrels, pulled up on the sand,
were opened up, men got drunk
and were fighting hand to hand.
There was fighting in the water,
a young boy joined as well;
he got drunk, his mother came
and cursed them all to Hell!

For a while the wreckage stayed there in the tide,
sails were taken to the fields and laid out to be dried.
They towed the broken vessel
to Falmouth, so they say,
Some wreck's still there at Pabyer Point
in Gorran Haven bay.

The brigantine then foundered on that fateful day.
The ship was broken on the Yaw in Gorran Haven bay.

Charlestown Harbour

Memories of an elderly man whose father had a sailing ship in around late 19th - early 20th century. The harbour was started in 1791 approx. The sailing ships brought in wood, grain, salt and coal and took back china clay and even ore. He remembered playing 'jumping from ship to ship' when there were 13 ships tied up - it was quite exciting!

Tucked along the Cornish coast well sheltered from the main
lies a pretty little port, Charlestown is its name;
but long before its hey-day, or as it's known today,
it bore the name of West Polmear with fishing in the bay.
People then were poor, and cottages were few,
and men would walk for many a mile
to find some work to do.
A man of vision there was, then, of Rashleigh family fame;
he lived at Menabilly House -
Charles was his Christian name.
He could see a harbour, hewn from cliff and shore,
where ships could berth in water deep
for loading clay and ore.

Then in seventeen ninety one work started on the dock.
They dynamited the hillside steep, for it was solid rock.
But, when completed, (and it was quite a feat),
a floating harbour they had made
with lock-gate and with leat.
Stately three-masted ships came from far-off seas;
often as many as thirteen ships
were crowded 'tween the quays.
Some brought coal for Cornish mines to fuel furnace flames,
from other climes then came the boats
with holds stocked full of grain.
Denmark sent the wooden staves for making barrels, strong;
salt, for salting pilchards down to keep them winter-long.

Down the hill from Stenalees came loads of China Clay;
the wooden drags were pulled behind
to slow the horse-drawn drays.
When they reached the gantry the work was hard and slow -
shovelling clay into the chutes to fill the holds below.
In the summertime they had Regatta days with silver bands
and kissing games for boys and maids to play!
Though many years have now passed by
since sailing ships were there,
and cargo boats no longer trade or tie up for repair,
but people in their hundreds come to see the history
of Charlestown, when a busy port, in the nineteenth century.

The Gentlemen

'The Gentlemen' were so called because they brought in contraband, mainly whiskey, cognac and tobacco, which could then be sold on. Many were involved including even the the gentry. When asked by Preventive Men if they knew anything about the haul they would say, "We stand aside and cover our eyes when the Gentlemen pass by!"

The Southern coast of Cornwall,
much battered by the waves,
was perfect for the smugglers
with many hidden caves.
The ships would come across from France
and 'stand-by' to the land,
to wait for when the coast was clear
to drop the contraband.

Many legends of their audacity,
tell us how the "Gentlemen" ran the smuggling industry!

In the inky darkness
the men were hidden there,
and long before the ship was seen
the bonfire was prepared.
They had to show great caution,
for there were penalties,
if they were caught while lighting fires,
to warn the ships at sea.

Whiskey came from Ireland,
brought by a daring crew.
brandy, fine, came o'er from France
and rum, in barrels, too.
Some ships brought tabaccy
and cognac ('cousin Jack').
China clay and even ore
were sometimes smuggled back.

20

The kegs were roped together
along the vessel's side,
then, were sunk into the sea,
to wait the evening tide.
Using covered paddles
men rowed them to the shore,
and hauled them up the steep cliff side
to take them to the store.

Local courts would offer
rewards of many pounds,
for information of the 'runs',
or where the goods were bound;
But, very few came forward,
their fellows to betray,
for even local "Gentry" then
were sharing in 'The Trade'!

Preventive Men would search them,
and say it was their 'duty',
but, locals knew, when it was stored,
that they'd share in the booty!
So, many awkward questions,
were given this reply,
"Just stand aside and cover your eyes,
when 'The Gentlemen' pass by!"

Many legends of their audacity,
tell us how the "Gentlemen" ran the smuggling industry!

Village Memories

These are a few memories of people who lived in Gorran Haven in the early - mid 20th century. It was a slower way of life and more sociable. Children played on their own on beaches, fields and cliffs - free as birds. I laughed when my mother-in-law (she had 4 sons) said in later life, "Oh, I always knew where my boys were!" My husband told me a different tale!

Pilchards roasting on the fire in a cottage by the sands,
Saffron cake, freshly baked, made by Cornish hands.
Waiting and anticipating, pasties to be done;
tempting whiffs, mixing with the smell of new yeast buns.

Simple ways and lazy days
when there was time to play.
These are village memories
of youthful yesterdays.

The church would have a village fête, & if the day was warm,
games of chance, we would dance on the vicarage lawn.
"Bowling for a pig" was played and many varied stalls
with "Guess the weight of the cake" - a social day for all.

Friday was the day to get the cricket pitch in trim;
practice night - get it right - then finish at the inn.
Ladies made the sandwiches and tea for all who came;
it was fun in the sun to see the local game.

Each year in the harbour when the winter storms were due,
fishermen, many then, had much work to do.
Inch by inch they wound the winch across the rising ground,
wire rope hauled the boats to safety in the pound.

Simple ways and lazy days
when there was time to play.
These are village memories
of youthful yesterdays.

Up upon the sunny cliffs near a rocky ledge,
two young lads having fun seeking seagull eggs!
Little did they ever think how changed their lives could be
if they slipped, lost their grip, and plunged into the sea!

Sometimes in the summertime,
a sports day would be planned -
on the beach, quite a treat, with racing on the sand.
There would be the greasy pole,
stuck well out from the quay,
pillow fight - get it right - then knock them in the sea!

Jumble sales were all the rage in the village hall;
bargains old, many sold, a ladies "free for all!"
Saturdays we dressed up for the "fifty-fifty" hop -
old and young, all would come,
we danced 'till we would drop.

Simple ways and lazy days
when there was time to play.
These are village memories
of youthful yesterdays.

The Early Tinners

The early tinners used to dig on their own and were called 'Streamers'. Later on, mines were dug and companies were formed. The wages were very poor and many were near starving so they caused riots to get to the cornstores. Eventually many tinners went off to California, South Africa and Australia to have a better life. Polgooth was one of the most important mining places in Cornwall and the country.

In early times there were so many tinners;
sometimes their luck held good when veins were new.
Disputes they had to settle in the Stannary Courts;
in Truro town they paid the taxes due.

Life was so short for the tinners then;
they were independent hard-working men.

Then came the richer merchants with the money;
the companies they formed were large and strong,
but the wages men were paid were very poor indeed,
and their life expectancy was not too long.

Some tinners still preferred to work 'on tribute', but
when veins ran out they had no food to eat,
so, they raided all the corn stores in the local market town
and caused a lot of riots in the street.

A later boom in tin brought work a-plenty,
with pumping stations driven now by steam,
and many mines were sunk below the level of the sea,
for they had to go far out to reach the seams.

Life was so short for the tinners then;
they were independent hard-working men.

But ore was found in other foreign places
and thousands of the tinners left our shores,
for the mines were closing down
and there was no work around,
so they went to seek their fortunes out abroad.

Now nearly all the tin mines are in ruins.
The broken chimneys stark against the sky;
but, some have been preserved to remind us of the past,
and the hardships of the mining days gone by.

Life was so short for the tinners then;
they were independent hard-working men.

The Little Cornish Ports

Just over 100 years ago standpipes were sometimes the only source of fresh, clean water to be had in villages. Women would meet there and it was very sociable (see page 42). Smuggling was rife 220 years ago - a necessary source of income to many. Preventive Men tried to keep it in hand - ineffectively! The little railway (now a track) was built solely to transport the china clay to Pentewan and coal was taken back to St Austell. They had to scrub out the wagon so the white clay could be put in the trucks - what a job!

I recall the slated cottages along the cobbled streets,
the water pump and standpipe, where women used to meet,
the menfolk in the harbour would prepare the fishing fleet;
that was life - in the little Cornish Ports.
The little fleets would leave the sheltered quay
at close of day,
and you could see their tiny lights out twinkling in the bay;
the pilchards in the 'hogsheads' were exported far away;
that was life - in the little Cornish Ports.

Smuggling was a way of life to many people then;
they'd plenty of good brandy and 'tabaccy' in the dens,
for the Mevagissey luggers could out-run Preventive Men!
that was life - in the little Cornish Ports.
In the Meva bakehouse run by Mr Way,
the ladies took their saffron cakes and pasties on a tray,
to bake them in the oven, just a penny they would pay;
that was life - in the little Cornish Ports.

The China Clay was taken to Pentewan on the train,
for loading on the larger ships who'd come across the main;
coal was packed into the trucks and taken back again;
that was life - in the little Cornish Ports.
The little local 'cobblers' working at the side
would take a rope to sailing schooners waiting for the tide,
for Pentewan harbour entrance really wasn't very wide;
that was life - in the little Cornish Ports.

The Gorran Haven boatyard where they were known so well
for making sturdy fishing boats
that they would sometimes sell
to Cornish in Australia - they wanted one as well;
that was life - in the little Cornish Ports.
The women worked beside the fire, making fishing nets,
then, took them to the barking house & left them to be set.
Now many of the cottages are used for summer 'lets' -
and that's life - in the little Cornish Ports.

The boatyards and the packing sheds
are yearly closing down.
The ports have many trippers
when the summertime comes around
and the shops are full of trinkets
that are made in Chinatown;
now that's life - in the little Cornish Ports.
Although the harbour's busy, the local people say
that many of the working men have had to move away
looking for employment but they may come back one day;
now that's life - in the little Cornish Ports.

A Winter Beach (Vault Beach)

When I lived at Gorran Haven I went for a walk on the 'Gruda' which is a wonderful walk before you get to the Dodman Point and then down to Vault Beach. It was in January and a cold, grey but bright, day and I really enjoyed the walk. I was the only one there and it was a wonderful experience.

Down on the path where it borders the sea
the damp grass lay.
Tranquil I stood
looking along
the lonely sweep of the bay.
I gazed a while on the waters below.
with a soft mist falling,
the only sound was seagulls calling.

Steep is the way to the white beach below
where winds blow free.
Cold, black the rocks,
jagged and bare,
reaching into the sea.
The tideline was high from the wild winter gales
with the seaweed drying
and tumbled driftwood lying.

Curling and rippling the waves rolled along
onto the shore.
Mingled with sand
and dappled in foam,
they fell back seaward once more.
Hazy and still was that wide open bay,
with the daylight fading
and only the seabirds wading.

I made a line with my footprints behind
along the sand.
Pebbles and shells
borne by the tide
shining bright in my hands.
Dove grey the sky on that cold winter sea
with a sharp wind sighing
and the last of the twilight dying.

Colours Of Cornwall

I used to paint and I loved the different colours in Cornwall - shades of ochre and bronze on the rocks; the colourful flowers growing on the cliffs even though they are blasted with gales, and the changing moorland tones as the year progressed and, most of all for me, the colours in the sea and shallows.

Down the country lanes,
scented bluebells colour the fresh spring day.
Ragged hawthorn trees
up on the banks
shaped by the wind -
framing the distant views of the tips of clay.
These are the colours I see, painting pictures, for me.

Up on the barren moors,
dainty heather bells give a purple hue.
Brown-grey the old tin mines;
yellow gorse
growing nearby.
In the far off haze the Atlantic blue.
These are the colours I see, painting pictures, for me.

Over the wind-tossed bay,
stretches of blue reflect in the moving tide.
Startling bright the cliffs
when caught by the sun -
sienna and grey.
Golden lichened rocks at the water side.
These are the colours I see, painting pictures, for me.

Skyline of cobalt blue;
gaily painted boats at the quay below.
Waving golden grass
with poppies of red,
montbretia too;
close to the edge the ox-eyed daises grow.
These are the colours I see, painting pictures, for me.

Floating seaweed hangs -
emerald green and brown it sways in the sea.
Down in the turquoise pools
mussels of black
cling to the rocks;
swirling oxide green, the waves break free.
These are the colours I see, painting pictures, for me.

Tucked in the sheltered lee,
purple veronicas nod in the cottage beds.
Over the stony walls
hydrangea heads of
white, pink and blue;
fuschia hedges hanging with teardrops, red.
These are the colours I see, painting pictures, for me.

Off To Australia

A widow was left with a son and two girls (maids) and no work to be had. Work for miners, carpenters, etc., was advertised to be had in Australia (Adelaide) with passage paid, so her son decided to go and seek their fortunes. Many never survived the journey and others were never heard of again. Some, however, did well, so this is her story.

Oi was left a widow poor,
with a son, two maids and a home no more!
There was no work to be 'ad around
because the mines was closing down.
Men left for America
and Australia.

We 'eard there was work in Adelaide
for strong young men and their passage paid!
Desperate we was for work, you know, and
so my son decided to go
to that continent so far
called Australia.

Oi cried as my son's ship left the quay,
'e said 'e'd come back for we.
For two long years we waited in vain,
then at last 'is letter came
from a place peculiar
way in Australia.

'E said the voyage took eighty days
cramped together in a dismal space.
Women and men - no privacy!
Then some died of the dysentery.
'E became a ship's carpenter
on his way to Australia.

The ship arrived and he thanked the Lord
with many sickly folk aboard.
'E said, "There's lots of work to do
for carpenters and miners too.
There's many mines in Kooringa
in south Australia.

'E worked 'ard every hour 'e could;
made 'is mark, as Oi knew 'e would.
'E said, "'E built a little place with
three good rooms and outdoor space;
'tis hotter than where you are,
here in Australia."

Then 'e met a pretty maid, said,
"We got married in Adelaide.
Kapunda is our little town -
with plenty of Cornish folk around.
It's a better life by far
so come to Australia!"

So 'ere we are on this clipper ship.
'E sent money to pay for the trip.
We've placed our lives in God's good grace,
tho' fearful we are of that 'furrin' place
and a land unfamiliar,
but, we'm off to Australia!

EMIGRATION
TO
SOUTH
AUSTRALIA

Her Majesty's Colonization Commis-
sioners having determined to dispatch in the
course of a few weeks a large number of Emi-
grants, all eligible persons may obtain, by
making an IMMEDIATE application, a

FREE
PASSAGE!

The classes of persons now in requisition are
Agricultural Laborers,
SHEPHERDS, CARPENTERS
BLACKSMITHS
AND
STONE MASONS
And all Persons connected with Building.
Application to be made to
Mr. I. LATIMER,
Rosewin-row, TRURO.

33

Bodmin Gaol

We went to have a look at Bodmin Gaol but didn't know what to expect. It was most interesting. We were told some of the tales of convicted felons and I could not get them out of my mind. The prison was given an award for being the most up to date example of a good prison (in the early 20th century) because it had hot water pipes running through the cells. But, oh, what a dismal place it must have been!

Just outside of Bodmin lies a building dark and grey;
it housed the thieves and murderers and felons of the day.
For murder, treason, arson, they lived in terror for -
they knew they'd hang when they walked through the door!
They knew the trap would open -
it would go down with a clang
and many people came to see them hanged!

Matthew was a labourer as ugly as could be,
he fancied pretty Charlotte but she didn't fancy 'e.
In a fit of fury he did her mortal harm,
they say her ghost still wanders on the farm!
Oh the trapdoor it fell open
and it went down with a clang
and they came from miles around to see him hanged.

A farmer's wife was angry, set her neighbour's hay alight;
when she was arrested, they thought she would get 'life',
but just for setting fire to a little mow of hay
she went to meet her Maker on that day!
For arson 'twas the penalty,
but few thought she would hang
but still the trapdoor went down with a clang.

The Lightfoot brothers' hanging - it was a grand affair!
The town was full to bustin', 'twas like a village fair!
They even stopped a local train so all could see their fate -
when they hanged them high above the Southern Gate.
The trapdoor it fell open
and it went down with a bang
and more than 20,000 watched them hang!

Rejected by the father, desperate and poor,
they said she killed her sickly baby up on Bodmin Moor;
they hanged her youthful body, to the coalyard it was bound
for she could not be laid in hallowed ground.
The trapdoor it fell open
and it went down with a clang;
'twas a cruel day when little Lizzie hanged!

They would hang for treason, highwaymen as well,
arsonists and murderers - all were in the cells,
but what if they were innocent? They had no hope at all -
when they cried for *justice* as they took the fall.
But the trapdoor it still opened
and it went down with a clang
and there was no retribution once they'd hanged!

Down Meva' Way

I got talking to an elderly lady, born and brought up in Mevagissey, and she was lamenting the way how life has changed and told me about her upbringing there around the early 20th century.

Oi was born in a little house that overlooked the quay,
and Oi could see the fishin' boats a-working out at sea.
We'd watch the men unload the fish they'd netted in the bay
and we would play upon the quay -
down Meva' way.

Oi'd help to clean and gut the fish in weather sometimes chill
preparing pilchards for the cans and we worked with a will.
The loaded mauns were sent to other markets in the bay
and oi was in love with a fisherman -
down Meva' way.

Down along the cobbled streets the happy people came -
dressed in all their Sunday best to see me
change moi name;
The preacher then 'e blessed us all
in the chapel quaint and grey,
The day Oi wed moi fisherman -
down Meva' way.

The times was hard and we was poor,
moi man, the babe and me.
In wintertime when seas was rough the boats still put to sea
and when the storms came suddenly
we could but wait and pray
that we'd still 'ave our fishermen -
down Meva' way.

And often in the summertime on evenings long and fair,
the choir would sing upon the quay and many folk was there
in June, at Mevagissey feast, a local band would play
and we would join the merry throng -
down Meva' way.

Now the harbour's full of pleasure craft,
expensive bright and new,
and since the trawler men have come the fish are very few;
some local boats they still go out for fishin' round the bay,
but we remember the way it was -
down Meva' way.

'E Bought A Mangle For Me!

I was told of a fisherman's family who lived in a 2-up/2-down cottage right by the quay. They had brought up 11 children in that house and his wife also took in some laundry to do. The problem was getting it dry!

When Oi was sixteen and pretty was Oi -
Ah! What a memory!
Oi met a fisherman sturdy and strong,
'andsome and merry.
Then we got wed and happy was we,
moi husband, his mother and me.
We 'ad a cottage, 'twas two up and down,
tucked away close by the sea.

Then we 'ad children, a fine little crew -
ever so many!
'E 'ad to work hard to keep us all fed,
it cost quite a penny.
A copper we 'ad in a shed out the back,
to do all the washin', you see,
but we had a problem to get it all dry,
then 'e bought an old mangle for me.

It had two rollers to squeeze out the wet
by winding the handle.
Women would pay a good penny to put
their sheets through moi mangle.
Oi'd salt away pennies each day;
'E'd sell 'is fish for the canning.
More children came, 'twas eleven in all -
it wasn't very good plannin'!

Then came the war and 'e went to enlist
to fight with his brothers.
Later we 'eard that 'is ship had gone down -
'E drowned with the others.
Though times was bad, Oi still had to work,
but Oi 'ad the mangle to help.
It earned me a crust to keep all of us
and bring up the children moi-self.

Now we do the laundry for many a house,
even the manor.
For washin' and dryin' and ironin' a sheet
we earn a tanner.
When I look back at the things that 'e did,
and 'e was a good man, you see,
Oi just want to say the best thing for me was
when 'e bought that mangle,
that old iron mangle,
when 'e bought that mangle for me!

*NB: a 'tanner' was the slang name for a sixpence which is
2½p today! For those who have never used a mangle - if
sheets etc. were folded wet and squeezed through the
rollers, which could be tightened, they came out just slightly
damp. It saved hours of labour and hanging on lines.*

Never A Miner I'll Be!

This is about a young boy in the 19th century whose family had always been miners. He had already started at the mines at about 8 years old and he hated the thought of having to go down the mines in a few years time.

Down, down, down to the bottom of the shaft
where there was no source of light,
moi father, like 'is father before 'im,
worked there the whole of 'is life.

Oi said, "'Tis not a good life
and 'tis not for me,
and never a miner I'll be."

Dark, dark, dark are the tunnels far below,
with only a candle to see,
'tis a long walk to reach the face,
sometimes out under the sea!

Hack, hack, hack in the dripping wet and dirt,
picking away at the ore;
with cramped and tired and aching limbs
for eight long hours or more.

Long, long, long are the ladders to climb -
sometimes they'd break - men would fall.
Lucky they were if damage was slight,
or if they survived it at all!

Work, work, working hard, moi father saved for me,
'till an apprenticeship 'e found,
so Oi became a carpenter in our town
and did never have to go underground.

Well, Oi said, "'Tis not a good life
and 'tis not for me,
and never a miner I'll be."

'E Said 'E'd Look After Me

So often we tend to romanticise the past when, in reality, it was pretty hard for most folk and grinding poverty for many, especially if they were left a widow with children.

Oi was a maid who knew little of life,
Oi met a miner who made me his wife.
'E was a streamer out diggin' for tin,
dirty the work and the profits was slim.
'E worked as hard as could be.
'E said 'e'd look after me.

He took a job with a mine company;
diggin' for tin way out under the sea.
Wages was poor - there was no work about -
who ever thought that the ore would run out!
And we 'ad children, all three.
'E said e'd take care of we.

Then mines was closing - no work to be found;
so many young miners was America bound.
'E took a place on an old packet ship,
used all our money to pay for the trip.
We cried as the ship left the quay.
'E said e'd come back for we.

Lately a letter was given to me,
told of a Packet gone down in the seas.
Valuable cargo was lost in the waves -
none of the people on board it was saved.
He promised a good life for me.
He'll never come back for we.

Oi 'ave no work and my health now is poor.
Hunger and poverty knocked at moi door.
Babes 'on the parish' but they'll have food to eat,
clothes on their bodies, some shoes on their feet!
Why did this happen to we?
Now it's the workhouse for me!

The Workhouse was where people were sent when they had nothing at all. The children were placed 'on the parish' which meant they had some education before being apprenticed out. Men, women and children were separated and saw little of each other. They were set to work breaking rocks or picking oakum, but, at least, they had food and shelter. Workhouses, which had provided poor relief since Elizabethan times, were only phased out in 1936.

"In Those Times"

Footwear in the 19th century was quite varied according to their uses and station. Ladies wore high-buttoned boots with many tiny buttons or hooks that took ages to do up. Paupers and widows, many of those from the mines, had to cover their feet with rags to keep out the cold, which was often made from sacking. Some types of boots are still worn today. The term 'slipper' means grimey in Cornish dialect.

High buttoned boots, latest black gown,
worn by the wife of the draper in town;
doing up all those buttons so fine,
dressing took quite a long time!

Heavy with clay, dusty and white,
worn at the clay pits by day and by night -
thick Darby Clogs for labourer's feet
made to keep out the heat.

Up on the mare on a saddle that shone,
richly embossed were the boots he had on,
calf leather gauntlets for warming his hands,
many mines on his land.

Fisherman's boots up to the thigh,
made for deep water to keep themselves dry,
treated with tar, linseed and lime,
'slipper' with blood, fish and grime.

44

Milking the cows, cutting the corn,
winter and summer the brown boots were worn;
leggings above, protective and strong,
laced with thin leather thongs.

Above the mine the wagons of tin
waited for children, cloth-footed and thin,
who worked with the women to sort out the ore,
began work at 8 years or more!

Old wooden clogs, clopping as she
hurried along to the fish cannery;
socks on her feet, thickened and old,
trying to keep out the cold!

In a dark hovel, desperate, in need,
a widow lays weeping with children to feed.
feet bound in linen, 'twas better than bare;
no husband - no one to care!

There in her carriage in fine silken hose,
a lady rides by in her velvety clothes;
slippers of kid and haughty young eye -
poverty passes her by!

Index

Poem Title or *Place Featured*	*Page*
A Summer's Eve	14
A Winter Beach (Vault Beach)	28
Bodmin	34
Bodmin Gaol	34
Bodmin Moor	34
Charlestown	4, 18
Charlestown Harbour	18
Cliff Primroses, Cornwall	9
Colours Of Cornwall	30
Down Meva' Way	36
'E Bought A Mangle For Me	38
'E Said 'E'd Look After Me	42
Fowey	4
Gorran Haven	14, 16, 22, 26, 28
In Those Times	44
Menabilly	18
Mevagissey	12, 26, 36, 38
Newquay	10
Never A Miner I'll Be	40
Off To Australia	32